Promoting LEADERS

Who Know How to Serve

Promoting LEADERS

Who Know How to Serve

DR. SHERRY GAITHER

Mall Publishing, Co.

THE PRINTED WORD THE PLANTED SEED

NILES, ILLINOIS

Published by:
Mall Publishing Company
5731 West Howard Street
Niles, Illinois 60714
877.203.2453

Cover Design: Andrew Ostrowski

Book Design: Marlon B. Villadiego

Unless otherwise indicated, Scripture is taken from the Holy Bible, the King James Version (KJV)

ISBN 0-9760362-2-3

For licensing / copyright information, for additional copies or for use in specialized settings contact:

Dr. Sherry Gaither
Stronghold Christian Church
724 Rock Chapel Road
Lithonia, Georgia 30058

www.strongholdcc.org
email: s.gaither@strongholdcc.org
Phone: 770.322.9010

DEDICATION

To my greatest cheerleader, my husband, Benjamin who continues to inspire me to complete my destiny. Thank you for being my partner in ministry. This project could not have been done without you.

TABLE OF CONTENTS

Dedication...v

Acknowledgements
I Give Thanks...ix

Foreword
Bishop Eddie Long..xi

Introduction..xiii

Chapter One
What's My Title?..1

Chapter Two
Cream Rises to the Top...5

Chapter Three
Leadership is not for Wimps..9

Chapter Four
Leadership According to Jesus...21

Chapter Five
I Am What I Do...33

Chapter Six
Microwave Promotion...39

Chapter Seven
Will the Real Leader Please Stand Up................................47

Chapter Eight
Can You Pass the Test?..53

Chapter Nine
An Attitude Adjustment..55

Chapter Ten
**Title and Position
or Performance and Productivity**......................................59

Chapter Eleven
Do You Have What it Takes?..63

Chapter Twelve
No Turning Back: *A Call to Commitment*.............................71

Chapter Thirteen
A Final Word..75

Afterword
Dr. LaFayette Scales..79

Notes..81

ACKNOWLEDGEMENTS
I GIVE THANKS

To Jordan, my dear son, you were born to lead. May God empower you to do his will.

To Min. Donna Carter, a true and faithful servant leader. You have been through the process; it's time for your promotion.

To the committed leaders and faithful members of Stronghold Christian Church, your prayers and loving support have been a blessing to me.

To my parents, George and Elizabeth Pinkett, your godly example is the foundation on which I stand.

FOREWORD
BISHOP EDDIE LONG

There are many leaders among us, but how many of them are servants? Jesus said He came to serve, not to be served. And furthermore, in Matthew 20:26 He said, "Whoever desires to become great among you, let him be your servant."

Let's go a step further. How many leaders are really qualified to hold the position indicated by their title? How many of them are intimately familiar with the vision they are to help make happen within the realm of that title? Unfortunately, throughout the Body of Christ, for many leaders, the answers to these questions are unsatisfactory.

Too often, we put leaders with inadequate training in positions, and then we do not follow through with accountability or evaluation. Inevitably the cycle of deadbeat leadership continues, crippling the Body of Christ, depriving thousands, even millions of much needed, wise leadership.

Effective leadership is paramount for the people of God. We are called to set standards for the world to follow, to set examples for relationships - whether business, political, personal or spiritual. The type of standards God wants us to exemplify requires top-notch leadership in all areas of life. They require longevity in servitude, sacrifice, unselfishness and commitment. Such standards must be embraced and placed within the church itself, especially amongst its leaders.

It's time for true leadership to arise, take on appropriate roles, and lead with Godly wisdom and authority. Such a leader has come to the forefront, and now, through her book, "Promoting Leaders - Who Know How To Serve," Dr. Sherry Gaither is willing to share the lessons she learned and teach the necessary principles leaders must possess today.

I had the pleasure and benefit of Dr. Sherry Gaither as a member of my staff. She was first a servant, and then a leader, submitted in authority, well qualified, and the producer of much fruit. She became an even greater leader as she took on the role of pastor along with her husband. From her experience in many leadership roles, Dr. Gaither gives us an inside look at what it means to be a leader, how to choose appropriate leaders, and how to maintain effective leaders in appropriate positions. In "Promoting Leaders - Who Know How To Serve," she digs out the root of leadership problems we face today, and not only that - she gives solutions. Absorb the knowledge within, and allow your leaders to reach new altitudes, that they may accomplish all God has set their hand to; that they may be effective leaders for His Kingdom.

Bishop Eddie L. Long
Senior Pastor
New Birth Missionary Baptist Church

INTRODUCTION

Have you noticed that in many of today's churches, titles and positions are the motivating factors for seeking positions? Far too many leaders are being promoted without prior experience or pre-leadership training. In fact in some cases, leaders are being recruited without having successful track records of faithfulness, commitment, or serving. According to Laurie Beth Jones, author of *Jesus Ceo*,

> No matter how "great" you are, if you believe that you have been called into leadership in the church, there must be a method or criteria for evaluating you

Jesus did not proceed with his working relationships until he knew where each person stood. Like all good leaders, he was looking for commitment from his staff. He deserved it, as does anyone who is willing to stand up for a cause.[1]

Too often, within our churches, leaders are chosen haphazardly. Individuals are quickly recruited, placed in positions, and given titles and responsibilities as a result of desperation, lack of time, or just lack of knowledge. Their effectiveness as servant leaders is based on "luck."

No matter how "great" you are, if you believe that you have been called into leadership in the church, there must be a method or criteria for evaluating you.

PROMOTING LEADERS-Who Know How to Serve has been birthed out of the frustration my husband and I experienced as pastors. Our ministry began as a Bible study in our home. As the ministry grew, the need for additional leaders increased. Initially there were no standard operating procedures for identifying and training leaders. Most leaders were drafted to fill newly created positions. Members motivated by titles and authority, eagerly accepted leadership positions. As the ministry grew, job descriptions were developed to provide direction and monthly leadership meetings were implemented to provide information, but not necessarily training.

> Today, I run from individuals who join our church and immediately look for the "fast track" promotion.

Inevitably, leadership challenges continued as a result of the ministry not having a process by which potential servant leaders were identified, and screened prior to them being placed into leadership positions. As the ministry continued to grow numerically, demands increased while leadership stability decreased. Several elders, ministers, deacons, and ministry leaders were released from positions for a variety of reasons. In an attempt to reduce the turnover of ministry leaders, we improved our training of individuals once they assumed leadership positions.

However, this method assumed that the individuals chosen to serve in the various positions possessed hearts both to serve and lead. There was nothing in place to evaluate their potential as leaders before they were given titles or authority. As a result, members continued to jockey for positions of importance without having a sense of true biblical servanthood.

Our experience has taught us that leadership training is more effective when it is implemented as one of the tools used to determine the criteria for potential leaders prior to them being promoted. Since that time we have developed training programs for every level of ministry.

Today, I run from individuals who join our church and immediately look for the "fast track" promotion. While we respect individuals for what they have accomplished, they must now show faithfulness in our ministry before we can "lay hands on them".

PROMOTING LEADERS-Who Know How to Serve is the cry of my heart and my desire to see our twenty-first century churches return to the biblical mandate of servant leadership. It is imperative that we understand the difference between having a title and a position and serving in a position.

However, there are two schools of thought when we find ourselves with a ministry vacancy to fill. One places the major emphasis on meeting the needs of the moment by filling ministry vacancies with "warm bodies" and for the most part, that's just what we do. Usually, it's not until you've been burned that you begin to realize the need to place the "right" people in the "right" positions according to their gifts, talents, and abilities.

I have several goals in writing this book. The first goal is to change our mind-set concerning the method by which individuals are promoted into leadership positions.

According to leadership expert, John Maxwell,

The key to making the right choice depends on two things: (1) your ability to see the big picture, and (2) your ability to judge potential employees during the selection process.[2]

In his book, *Developing the Leader Around You*, Maxwell stated that he starts with an inventory called the Five A's. By answering these five questions he is then in a better position to recruit leaders.

- What is the need (assessment)?
- Who is already on board (assets on hand)?
- Are they qualified (ability)?
- Are they willing (attitude)?
- What have they done so far (accomplishments)?

From a biblical perspective, Jesus used a very simplistic method to recruit His disciples, "Come, ye after me, and I will make you to become fishers of men" (Mark 1:17). However, Jesus was no fool, He knew the importance of qualifying the disciples. The very basic definition of a disciple is a disciplined follower of the beliefs and practices of the one who disciples him.

To see how real and committed they were, He tested them repeatedly. Their faith was tested when He allowed them to cross the lake in a tiny boat. Their obedience was tested when He asked them to find enough bread to feed four thousand. Their submission was tested when He asked them to leave their families and occupations to follow Him. Their prayer life was tested when He asked them to pray with Him for one hour.

> The problem we encounter in the Body of Christ is too many believers want the benefits of promotion without the rigor of the process.

My second goal is to encourage a paradigm shift in leadership recruitment. I believe that the development and promotion of a pre-leadership training class will influence how leaders are selected. In addition, a training program will also help to shape the philosophy of current leaders and provide a biblical foundation for those who have been given titles, but have never been formally trained as servant-leaders.

Let's be honest, every church should provide and every leader should desire a program of formal training prior to assuming a leadership position. While we understand that Christian leadership involves a supernatural empowerment from God, servant-leadership is a gift to be cultivated through training. The problem we encounter in the Body of Christ is too many believers want the benefits of promotion without the rigor of the process.

How then, do you identify and recruit servant leaders? You might be led to think that focusing on the traits of out-standing leaders would offer a "sure" method. Others might suggest that leaders are produced by placing them in situations that allow for them to rise to the occasion. And there are those who would recommend proving leaders by observing their track record.

With all that in mind, the final goal of this book is to offer tools to aid in assessing the faithfulness, commitment, and servant attitude of aspiring leaders. For your convenience I have included a leadership assessment guide and eight leadership lessons to be used in a pre-leadership training class. While selecting the right individuals for the appropriate positions is time-consuming and no easy task, the long-term benefits of recruiting servant leaders are numerous.

CHAPTER ONE

WHAT'S MY TITLE?

How many times have you met people whose only agenda was to "climb" the church ladder? The corporate mindset has invaded many in today's churches with the notion that leaders are to be served based upon their conferred titles and positions. Over the years, the balance between serving and being served has become out of balance. I believe that God is requiring the Church to return to the biblical mandate set by Jesus Christ.

From a biblical perspective, what does it mean to be a servant-leader? The answer to this question can be found in the twentieth chapter of Matthew. But Jesus called them unto him and said; Ye know that the princes of the Gentiles exercise dominion over them, and they that are great exercise authority upon them. But it shall not be so among you:

but whosoever will be great among you, let him be your minister. And whosoever will be chief among you, let him be your servant. Even as the Son of man came not to be ministered unto but to minister, and to give his life a ransom for many, (Matt 20:25-28).

Jesus spoke mainly of diakoneo, serving one another. The Bible states that Jesus humbled Himself and took on the form of a servant. A bond-servant is the complete opposite of the term, Lord, a title by which believers will one day recognize the risen and exalted Christ (Phil 2:7). While servanthood was not on the minds of the disciples, Jesus set an example for all believers by washing the feet of the disciples before the Feast of the Passover (John 13:1-17).

> Over the years, the balance between serving and being served has become out of balance.

Kortright Davis, author of *Serving with Power* states,

Our ecclesial traditions have not always been clear about whether we really mean "service," or whether we mean "authority," or "power," or even "duty." When Jesus of Nazareth uses the term in the gospel story, he clearly renounces any sense of power or authority, and gives himself unconditionally to that self-sacrificing life of service and obedience to the God whom he calls "Father." His is a life of serving with power.[3]

The challenge before us in this generation, is how do we choose individuals to serve in leadership capacities? We must be willing to take a proactive approach to addressing the problem of identifying, recruiting, and qualifying servant leaders.

There are several ways to respond to the challenge. The first response to this problem is to educate ministry leaders, lay leaders, and laity concerning a biblical understanding of servant leadership in the Church and the biblical method by which servant-leaders should be chosen.

The term "servant" has changed grammatically and theologically since the early Church. Grammatically, the term servant was used in response to anyone who served. Over time, the word was used to refer to the name, title, or position of an individual. Theologically, in the early Church every believer was called to serve. The theological meaning of the word did not apply to an "elite" group of believers. Over a period of time the verb "serve" has become a noun, "servant" for positional-minded people whose ambition is not to serve, but to be served.

In addition, many of the instructions that Paul gave Timothy concerning the recruitment of deacons should also be used in recruiting leaders; "And let these also first be proved; then let them use the office of a deacon, being found blameless," (1 Tim 3:10). In 2 Tim 2:2, Paul further commands Timothy to commit the Word to faithful servants. One of our first considerations should be to promote individuals who have established a track record of faithfulness in serving where they are. Now faithfulness encompasses more than just dependability; it includes capability and skill level. I remember the story of a dear church sister who faithfully played the piano for over thirty-five years. Without fail, she was dependable and consistent; she consistently played every song in the same key.

The second response is a radical departure from conferring titles and positions. Can believers serve faithfully without titles of authority? I remember reading an article several years ago that was entitled: "What's in a Title?" Without realizing it, most people base their self worth on their ability to obtain titles or positions, so their primary goal is to increase their self-esteem by obtaining leadership positions. When was the last time you heard a believer sincerely declare, "I don't care about a title, I just want to serve"?

The third response is to develop a "pre-leadership" training program in which potential leaders are evaluated for faithfulness, commitment and ability, prior to their promotion into positions of authority. Think about it, isn't the foundation of ministry, people development? The idea is to place individuals in positions that can be immediate assets and not liabilities.

CHAPTER TWO

CREAM RISES TO THE TOP

While there is no fail-proof way to identify a potential servant leader, there are some criteria that can be used to aid in the process. Here is what Hanz Finzel, author of *Empowered Leaders* had to say,

Someone has said that leadership, like cream, rises to the top. Often leadership is not something a person volunteers for. It is something a person is chosen for by others as he or she rises through the ranks. So why is someone chosen to lead? What are the characteristics, skills, abilities, and personality that cause people to be selected for leadership?[4]

First, servant leaders are individuals who understand the vision of the organization and their role as ser-

vant leaders. I teach leadership classes in one of our local Bible colleges. Recently I put several students on the "hot

> Potential leaders should be looking for opportunities that are not necessarily in the limelight.

seat" by asking them to articulate the vision of the church they were a part of. Sadly, only one with hesitation could express the vision that she was charged to carry out. The question is: how can you adequately support a vision that you're not familiar with? Let's take that a step further: you are of no value to an organization until you understand the heart of that organization and the role you play in the organization.

Effective leaders are able to articulate the mission of the organization and the importance of fulfilling the vision.

Second, a servant leader will readily volunteer when needed. When my husband gets frustrated with our leaders, he constantly reminds me of how it was when he was aspiring to serve in ministry. His boot camp days began in the church parking lot, he was then promoted to cleaning the church bathrooms, and after a time of faithfully attending to the needs of others, he was given an opportunity to demonstrate his ability to serve in Sunday school.

Too many of God's beautiful people want to avoid the process of becoming servant leaders.

Potential leaders should be looking for opportunities that are not necessarily in the limelight. When a volunteer avoids small responsibilities or menial tasks, it is an indication that he lacks a servant's heart.

Let's now deal with the "A" words - authority and accountability. For some reason, believers have a problem submitting to authority and being held accountable. It appears that in the corporate arena we show more respect to those in authority than we do in the Church. Let me give you an example: we ask our leaders to contact the church in advance when they are unable to make leadership team meetings or other required events. Without fail, there are always leaders who are AWOL. So accountability must be the third criteria for identifying potential servant leaders. Since spiritual accountability is paramount for effective leadership, an individual who is unwilling to follow standard operating procedures is not a candidate for servant leadership.

Equally as important, successful leaders should be able to interact well with others and develop relationships on various levels. Let's face it, if you don't like dealing with people, you shouldn't be in leadership. We're not looking for data entry skills or computer experience. The job description reads: must be able to work with, relate to, and guide multiple personality types (and sometimes individuals with multiple personalities). Successful leaders recognize the power of being connected. As you read this book, think about someone whom you feel has the potential to be leader. How does he or she interact with others? Is he unapproachable? Does she possess exceptional people skills?

Finally, a proven track record is a useful indication of one's potential. Although one's history of serving is no indication of one's faithfulness in the future, it can offer insight into an individual's involvement in a given organization. One of the ways we test individuals is to give them assignments or opportunities to demonstrate their level of commitment and stick-to-itiveness (I like that word). The problem is, over a period of time, very few people "stick with it", which is the very reason you shouldn't be quick to promote individuals.

CHAPTER THREE

LEADERSHIP IS NOT FOR WIMPS:

AN OLD TESTAMENT VIEW

Moses, a Friend of God

And Israel saw that great work which the Lord did upon the Egyptians: and the people feared the Lord, and believed the Lord, and his servant Moses (Exod 14:31).

Moses, who was called the servant of God, had a unique relationship with the Lord, "And there arose not a prophet since in Israel like unto Moses, whom the Lord knew face to face," (Deut 34:10). Moses answered the call to leadership while on the backside of the desert. "Come now therefore, and I will send thee unto Pharoah that thou mayest bring forth my people, the children of Israel, out of Egypt" (Exod 3:10).

You can gain a valuable lesson from the way Moses responded to the call of God. Even though Moses acknowledged that he was there to serve God, he questioned how God could use him to deliver His people. "And Moses said unto God, 'Who am I, that I should go unto Pharoah and that I should bring forth the children of Israel out of Egypt?" (Exod 3:11)

Over the years I have watched individuals declare that they are ready to be used as God's man or woman of power. For the most part, their call may be genuine, but they have yet to understand the process by which God prepares us to complete our assignments. Most people, who "think" they're ready, determine their readiness based upon their scholastic accomplishments and innate abilities without relying on the empowering Presence of the Holy Spirit.

> When God calls you and you know that God's hand is upon you; you can endure the wilderness, walk through the valley of death, and survive the storms.

In an on-going dialogue with God, Moses continued to question his own leadership ability. He feared the Israelites would reject him as their leader and they would not believe that he was capable of delivering them. He also felt he lacked the oratory skills necessary to address Pharaoh, which left him feeling inferior. In his final response to the call of God, he accused God of not acting on his behalf.

Moses led the Israelites through the wilderness to Mt. Sinai, in obedience to the Lord. As the servant of the Lord, Moses taught the people what God expected of them; they were to be a holy people, separated unto God. As God's mouthpiece, Moses gave the Ten Commandments to the people. Under his leadership the children of Israel reached the borders of Canaan (Deut 32:1-43). When God calls you and you know that God's hand is upon you; you can endure the wilderness, walk through the valley of death, and survive the storms.

Jim McGuiggan, author of *The God of the Towel,* offers further insight as to Moses' job description,

Besides being a lawgiver, Moses was also the one through whom God presented the Tabernacle and instructions for the Holy office of the priesthood. Under God's instruction, Moses issued ordinances to cover specific situations, instituted a system of judges and hearings in civil cases, and regulated the religious and ceremonial services of worship.[5]

Through studying the life of the servant-leader Moses, we can learn the following four principles.

1. God humbles His servant so that he will obey, "Come now therefore, and I will send thee unto Pharaoh that thou mayest bring forth my people, the children of Israel, out of Egypt" (Exod 3:10). IF

you're still in a debate with God about your assignment, you're a prime candidate for my class, Leadership 101-Counting the Cost. One of the first Scriptures we quote is Galatians 2:20, in which the Apostle Paul declares that he has been bought with a price and no longer lives for himself. If you're not willing to die to your own will and your own agenda-you're not ready to lead!

2. Servant-leaders are not self-sent, self-made, or self-empowered (Exod 3:14). I teach a leadership class entitled: Dynamics of Biblical Leadership, which examines how God called, prepared, and qualified His leaders throughout the Bible. On the first day of class we discuss the necessity of knowing whether one's call was a genuine call from God, influenced by man, or self-promoted.

3. Leadership is not based upon academic knowledge, skill training, or giftedness; obedience and dependency is paramount to God (Exod 4:10). Every May prior to graduation, I bust the bubble of every graduating senior, by reminding him or her that his or her degree is not intended to take the place of the anointing of God. Most could care less about the anointing; they're more interested in financial compensation.

4.   A servant-leader must recognize that his position is based upon the plans of God according to His timing (Exod 5:21-22).   It's ok to read about Moses spending forty years in the palace, an additional forty years on the backside of a mountain, only to end with forty years in the wilderness-but that was Moses, not me!

Joshua, a Faithful Armor-bearer

"And Moses rose up, and his minister Joshua and Moses went up into the mount of God" (Exod 24:13).

God called Joshua to be a servant-leader to Moses. Moses appointed Joshua to be commander over the army to defend Israel.   It was Moses' job to intercede and Joshua's assignment was to fight, "So Joshua did as Moses had said to him, and fought with Amalek: and Moses, Aaron, and Hur went up to the top of the hill" (Exod 17:10).

> Every pastor dreams of having a "Joshua", a man or a woman whose loyalty and commitment is unwavering.

Now, for just a moment, take off your spiritual hat and place yourself in Joshua's shoes.   You're in the line of fire, battling for your life and you look up and see your leader way up in the nosebleed section.   To make matters worst, you're suffering from battle fatigue, but he's the one who needs help holding up his arms!   The question is- do you stop fighting and start complaining, or do you stick to the plan and complete the mission?

Joshua exemplified great courage as a warrior against the Amalakite, but he also demonstrated his faithfulness as a servant to Moses on Mt. Sinai. For forty days Joshua remained stationed on the side of the mountain waiting for Moses to return from his visitation with God (Exod 24:18).

Every pastor dreams of having a "Joshua", a man or a woman whose loyalty and commitment is unwavering. Be honest, how many days would you have stayed in the cliff of a mountain with no cell phone, pager, or fast food restaurant, not to mention television, satellite and remote. On a serious note, Joshua had no way of knowing whether Moses was ever coming back, but the Bible never portrays him as becoming double-minded or discouraged.

When Moses sent spies to scout out the land of Canaan, Joshua was selected as one of the twelve representatives. Although all of the spies agreed that the Promised Land was a land to be desired, ten spies complained that they were unable to possess it. Only Joshua and Caleb returned to the camp with a positive report that they could conquer it.

Getting potential leaders to understand visionary leadership can be challenging. Visionaries are motivated by faith to blaze trails even in the wake of evil reports. We preach faith, but we generally operate by what we see and how we feel. As a result of their demonstration of faith, Joshua and Caleb were able to enter into the Promised Land (Num 14:30).

Is there any doubt as to why the servant-leader, Joshua, was chosen to succeed Moses? God put Joshua through a rigorous leadership-training program with no guarantees that he would be promoted. Moses had led the children of Israel out of Egypt; Joshua's assignment was to lead them into Canaan.

"Moses my servant is dead; now therefore arise, go over this Jordan, thou and all this people, unto the land which I do give to them, even to the children of Israel. Every place that the sole of your foot shall tread upon, that have I given unto you, as I said unto Moses," (Josh 1:2,3).

A glimpse at the life of Joshua allows us to recognize the role of a servant-leader.

1. Leadership is progressive. Joshua began as a warrior, but through his obedient service, he became commander and chief (Exod 17:9-11).

2. Leadership is faithfully serving at one's current post despite distractions of others (Exod 32:17).

3. Servant-leaders are often rejected by those closest to them (Num 14:6-12).

4. Leadership responsibility is based upon submission to authority and faithfulness.

5. Leadership responsibility should be given gradually (Num 27:20).

6. Servant-leadership requires obedience at every command (Josh 6:1-20).

Joshua spent a considerable amount of time with Moses, so we can assume that he saw the other side of the man, i.e. his weaknesses, his issues, and his character flaws. Yet the Bible never shows Joshua disrespecting Moses, judging Moses, or exposing him to others.

David, a Servant After God's Heart

"Now then do it: for the Lord hath spoken of David, saying, By the hand of my servant David I will save my people Israel out of the hand of the Philistines, and out of the hand of all their enemies," (2 Sam 3:18).

David, the second king of Israel, began his leadership career as a keeper of his father's sheep (1 Sam 16:11). What appeared to be a menial task provided him with an opportunity to demonstrate his courage and faithfulness by killing both a lion and a bear (1 Sam 17:34-36). Listen, if you've been complaining that what you're presently doing in ministry isn't fulfilling your aspirations, could it be that you're being tested for future opportunities? You've heard the saying, "don't despise small beginnings".

Although he was anointed to be king at a young age, David's primary responsibility after he was anointed was as a shepherd and musician for King Saul (1 Sam 16:23). Let's unpack that statement.

> Some giants are the stepping-stones for your next promotion.

Most believers have never been taught that when they receive a prophetic word, an interpretation of a dream, or a confirmation of an anointing-this does not necessarily mean that they are ready to go to the next level. For most of us, it is the beginning of intense training. This was the case for David.

The servant-leader, David, demonstrated his abilities as a warrior when he answered the challenge of the giant, Goliath.

David became a hero when he defeated Goliath and regained national respect for the God of Israel (1 Sam 18:6). Some giants are the stepping-stones for your next promotion. One key piece of advice: you will never conquer anything if you keep running from it.

David continued to serve King Saul until Saul's jealousy forced him to flee as a fugitive (1 Sam 23:28; 24:1). I might as well be honest, everyone is not going to celebrate your victories and accomplishments-get use to it! But God will hold you accountable for the manner in which you conducted yourself, but you have no control over the reactions of others to your success.

At the death of King Saul, David was anointed King of Judah (2 Sam 2:1-4). David's rulership grew stronger because he was a faithful servant-leader, while Saul's kingdom grew weaker. David's third anointing as king came at the age of thirty. As king over all of Israel, he began to unite the kingdom.

Let's look at what we can glean from the life of David, the servant-leader.

1. David was faithful and obedient to the menial tasks that were given to him. "And Jesse said unto David, his son, 'Take now for thy brethren an ephah of this parched corn, and these ten loaves, and run to the camp to thy brethren,'" (1 Sam 17:17).

2. Servant-leadership has a tendency of stretching a leader. David served in three capacities at the same time: as armor-bearer, musician, and shepherd (1 Sam 16:21-23; 17:20).

3. Take note of how David exemplified wisdom when he was promoted to a greater position as commander.

"And David went out whithersoever Saul sent him and behaved himself wisely and Saul set him over the men of war and he was accepted in the sight of all the people and also in the sight of Saul's servants," (1 Sam 18:5).

4. David showed himself to be a faithful servant leader who did not retaliate against Saul, but he chose to honor his position as King of Israel despite Saul's continual threats.

"And he said unto his men, The Lord forbid that I should do this thing unto my master, the Lord's anointed, to stretch forth mine hand against him, seeing he is the anointed of the Lord," (1 Sam 24:6).

Elisha, a Servant with a Double Portion

"Then he arose and went after Elijah and ministered unto him," (1 Kings 19:21).

Elisha answered the call to become a servant leader while plowing in the field. His training and preparation came as a result of faithfully walking in the footsteps of his master Elijah. Elisha proved faithful throughout the mentoring process. Based upon his faithful service he received a double portion of his master's anointing.

Servant leadership at its best is portrayed through the life of Elisha.

1. A prerequisite for servant-leadership is faithfulness in one's present position. When Elijah found Elisha, the servant, Elisha was plowing the field (1 Kings 19:19).

2. A servant leader must be willing to sacrifice his personal ambitions in order to serve. Elisha left his career, parents, and community to serve Elijah (1 Kings 19:20).

3. As a servant leader, Elisha humbled himself to become one of Elijah's many student prophets. A leader cannot allow pride to keep him from obeying God's voice.

4. Elisha was faithful to complete his assignment under Elijah, which positioned him to be his successor (2 Kings 2:9-12).

CHAPTER FOUR

LEADERSHIP ACCORDING TO JESUS

From a biblical perspective, what does it mean to be a servant-leader? The New Testament describes the term "to serve" by at least eight different words. Let's study them: (1) diakonos (Acts 6:2), to serve at tables; (2) doulos (Luke 16:13), to serve as a bondslave; (3) latreuo (Matt 4:10), to serve for wages; (4) hypereto (Acts 13:36), to serve as a rower; (5) paredreuo (1 Cor 9:13), to serve as one who sits by constantly; (6) therapon (Acts 17:25), one who renders service without regard to being slave or free; (7) prosecho (Heb 7:13), to serve attentively; and (8) leitourgeo (Heb 10:11), to serve the church.

Servant Leader According to Jesus

"But it shall not be so among you: but whosoever will

be great among you, let him be your minister; and whosoever will be chief among you, let him be your servant. Even
as the Son of man came not to be ministered unto, but to
minister, and to give his life as a ransom for many" (Matt
20:26-28).

Matthew 20:25-28 is the reply Jesus gave when
responding to the request of James' and John's mother to let
her sons have positions of honor in the kingdom. Greatness
in the eyes of Jesus consisted not in having dominion over
people but in serving people.

Jim McGuiggan, author of *The God of the Towel*, stated,

*There are only two kinds of power or authority: pagan
and Christ-like. One is seized and is self-serving; the other
is bestowed and is other-serving. In Matthew 20, the Son of
Man is asking us: "How do you feel about those you wish to
have power over. What do you mean to do for them? Are
you willing to let serving them be your way of life and your
credentials for office?*[6]

In His discourse with the disciples Jesus makes a dis-
tinction between "the great" and "chief". The great were
those who committed themselves to minister. To be considered chief (protos), one would have to become as a servant
or bond-slave (doulos).

In the eyes of Jesus, the bond-slave is held in higher

esteem than the minister because one's commitment determines his status and reward. One who ministers may serve occasionally, while the service of a bond-slave is twenty-four hours a day, seven days a week. According to Gayle D. Erwin, author of *The Jesus Style*,

When Jesus alludes to submission, it is always directed toward leaders or the ones who want to be great in the kingdom and they are always ordered to submit downward, not upward.[7]

To His position-minded disciples, leadership in the Messiah's kingdom was the restoration of Israel as an earthly nation with power. They measured power by recognition, authority, dominion, and position.

T.W. Mason, author of *The Servant-Messiah* offers this insight,

We can see this definition worked out in detail in the words and deeds of the Ministry. In particular, it appears clearly in the sayings about the Son of Man, especially those, which emphasize his task of service and sacrifice. Along with these go the closely parallel sayings on the task of the disciples and the nature of the power and glory that they may hope to achieve.[8]

Serving the Will of God
Was His Eternal Aspiration.

"Jesus saith unto them, 'My meat is to do the will of Him who sent me, and to finish His work,'" (John 4:34).

The disciples of Jesus had just returned from buying food in the town. Their concern as to why Jesus was not eating prompted Him to explain the mentality of a servant-leader. Jesus explained that His passion and desire was to complete His assignment. His priority was the will of God for He recognized that God sent him. God expected Him to be obedient, faithful, and submissive. In a later discourse He reemphasized His purpose as a servant-leader (John 5:30).

Serving the Only True God
Was His Focus.

"Neither be ye called masters: for one is your Master, even Christ. But he that is greatest among you shall be your servant. And whosoever shall exalt himself shall be abased; and he that shall humble himself shall be exalted," (Matt 23:10-12).

This discourse to both the multitude and the disciples took place two days after Jesus had been escorted into town by thousands proclaiming Him to be the Messiah. He had demonstrated His authority by casting out the moneychangers. Through His teaching and healing He demonstrated His power. Both religious and government leaders felt threatened by His power and popularity. At risk were their leadership position, power, wealth, and security. Their only defense was to discredit Jesus through challenging questions. He responded by warning them against the danger of serving false religions.

The Scribes and Pharisees loved positions of honor, special seating, and places of recognition. Jesus declared that they were hypocrites; leaders who loved having titles and positions. Jesus pointed to Himself as their Master and God as their

> I have a real problem with individuals who think so highly of themselves that they cannot relate to the issues that others are struggling with.

Father. They were all to be considered servants of the Master, each to serve and help one another. According to Jesus, greatness should be measured by service, not by titles and positions.

Serving by Standards
Was His Objective.

"No servant can serve two masters: for either he will hate the one, and love the other; or else he will hold to the one, and despise the other. Ye cannot serve God and mammon," (Luke 16:13).

Jesus set a standard by which servant-leadership must be measured. He demonstrated for us that in his position of honor and majesty, He could be "touched". The principle of humility is the standard for servant-leadership. Consider these verses from the Book of Philippians:

"But made of himself of no reputation, and took upon him the form of a servant, and was made in the likeness of men and being found in fashion as a man, he humbled himself and became obedient unto death, even the death of the cross," (Phil 2:7,8).

I have a real problem with individuals who think so highly of themselves that they cannot relate to the issues that others are struggling with. When I'm hurting, I don't need someone who can just quote Scriptures to me...I'm looking for someone who will meet me at my point of need and walk with me.

> Ministry is about
> S-A-C-R-F-I-C-E,
> not STARDOM

Jesus was obedient and submitted to the will of the Father. He did not come to the earth as a great leader; He came as a servant to serve. According to author, Frank Damazio,

A leader, most people would say, is a person, who directs, administrates, organizes, makes decisions, delegates responsibilities, and plans for the future. This defini-

tion lacks a very essential part of true leadership: a leader is one who serves. A leader of God's people must have the inner attitudes and motivations, and the outer service, of a servant.[9]

The principle of dependency became a standard for servant-leadership. Christ's total dependency upon the Father is exemplified throughout the Gospels. "I can of mine own self do nothing: as I hear, I judge: and my judgment is just; because I seek not my own will, but the will of the Father which hath sent me," (John 5:30).

It's dangerous for a leader to think that he's all that and "a bag of chips". We have a son who has shown great potential in basketball and baseball. I am constantly reminding him (like a broken record) that his abilities and skills are a gift from God. Before every game, we pray that God will give him the ability to hit, throw, catch, jump, and make lay-ups, pass, and ultimately win! But at the end of the day, his assignment is to be vessel for the glory of God.

What Jesus wanted the Pharisees to grasp, was the concept of relationship to the Father. Jesus declared that they were hypocrites - leaders who loved having titles and positions. Jesus pointed to Himself as their Master and God as their Father. They were all to be considered servants of the Master, each to serve and complete an assignment.

The principle of sacrifice became the standard for servant-leadership. As Jesus shared His purpose and His fate with His followers, some were offended by what He said. "When Jesus knew in himself that his disciples murmured at it, he said unto them, Doth this offend you?" (John 6:61). Just imagine being a part of Jesus' entourage, to be known as "one of the boys", to be invited to weddings and dinners.

The disciples (remember the seventy) loved the fanfare. The problem is, if we get caught up with the benefits, we can forget about the cost. Jesus knew this, so He said it's time for a "reality-check", there's another side to ministry. Ministry is about sacrifice, not stardom.

The sacrifice to walk as a servant-leader caused many of His followers to waver and walk away. In the midst of His teachings, He turned to His faithful disciples and questioned their loyalty, "Then said Jesus unto the twelve, Will ye also go away?" (John 6:67).

I can't tell you the number of people who have said to my husband, "I've got your back, I'm with you all the way", but where are they now? Believers who are not willing to make sacrifices will always declare, "My season is up".

Serving by Transforming Others Was His Passion.

Leighton Ford author of Leaders on Leadership describes how Jesus transformed the disciples into leaders.

His six-step process was more of a life transformation than a program.

1. He called them individually and affirmed them.

2. He understood their strengths and weaknesses by building a relationship with them.

3. Third, He made them a team by balancing their abilities with their individual destinies and the overall vision.

4. He mentored and modeled His teachings for them, entrusting them to follow in His footsteps.

5. He tested them to reinforce their dependency upon God. During this stage, He separated them and began to invest more time in character development.

6. He empowered them, ordained them, and sent them out.

Serving by Example
Was His Model

"He riseth from supper and laid aside his garment; and took a towel and girded himself. After that he poureth water into a basin and began to wash the disciple's feet and to wipe them with the towel wherewith he was girded," (John 13:4,5).

The Bible states that Jesus humbled Himself and took on the form of a servant. A bondservant is the complete opposite of the term Lord, a title by which believers will one day recognize the risen and exalted Christ (Phil 2:7).

> Leaders don't audition for the role; they set an example by living the role of a servant leader.

While servanthood was not on the minds of the disciples, Jesus set an example for all believers when He washed the feet of the disciples before the Feast of the Passover. When Jesus "laid aside his garment," in essence He was stripping Himself of His glorious position as the Son of God, (Phil 2:6,7).

I almost believe that promotion ruins some believers. They work so faithfully before they are placed in authority and forget what it means to serve now that they have a title. Leaders don't audition for the role; they set an example by living the role of a servant leader.

Jesus knew who He was, therefore as Master, he could act like a slave; as the Highest, He could take the place of the lowest; and as the Sovereign, He could become the submissive.

According to author Jim McGuiggan,

Jesus knew he was going back to the Father-this was his divine destination. He knew he faced treachery, humiliation, desertion, and the Cross-, but he also knew that he would return to glory with his Father. In light of all this, knowing all this, and having loved his disciples from the beginning unto now-what did he do? He acted out servanthood.[10]

Jesus became a slave (doulos). His motive was to demonstrate that there was honor to be gained from serving others. In biblical days, most people wore sandals and their feet became extremely

> His motive was to demonstrate that there was honor to be gained from serving others

dirty. Upon entering a person's home, the poor would wash their own feet and the rich would have a servant to wash their feet. Jesus took upon Himself the form of a servant. It was not an act or a new ceremony, it was an attitude.

Serving by Love
Was His Foundation

"By this shall all men know that ye are my disciples, if ye have love one to another," (John 13:35).

The disciples had just been arguing over who should receive the highest positions of authority in the Kingdom of God (Luke 22:24-30). In the midst of their division, Jesus began to make profound statements concerning the future.

As the Son of Man, He became the Servant of all men and now He was about to become the sacrifice for all humanity (John 12:23,24).

Author, Gayle D. Erwin describes leadership through the eyes of love,

God and his Son are servants, examples, humble, as a child, as the younger, as the last, as the least, using no force, emptying itself. These traits that totally speak love were guiding principles, even commands, for the life of Jesus. Jesus was obedient to this servant love of man even in Gethsemane when the cost was going up astronomically.[11]

The commandment was new because it was a sacrificial love based upon obedience. The commandment was challenging because it required them to embrace others. The commandment was powerful because it was a sign to the world and to believers that they were followers of Christ.

One of the challenges we face as leaders is remembering that the Church is a spiritual hospital and people have issues. The Bible declares that love covers a multitude of sins, but as leaders we seem to expect members to be saved, delivered, and set free before they step foot in the Church. Thank God that Jesus could look beyond the Simon Peter that he recruited to see the Apostle Peter he became.

CHAPTER FIVE

PAUL:
I AM WHAT I DO

More than any other disciple or apostle, Paul is considered the most influential
teacher of Christianity. His
transformed life and missionary accomplishments serve as
a timeless example of a ser-

> The word "doulos" refers
> to a slave totally possessed
> by a master

vant-leader. In three different epistles he addresses himself
as the servant of Christ and once as a prisoner of Christ
Jesus. To Paul, servant-leadership was the highest call one
could answer.

Paul Developed a Slave Mentality

In the first chapter of Romans, Paul identifies himself
first as "a doulos" of Christ Jesus, "Paul, a servant of Jesus

Christ, called to be an apostle, separated unto the gospel of God" (Rom 1:1). The word "doulos" refers to a slave totally possessed by a master.

Paul was identifying himself with the slave market of his day in which a slave was purchased and existed to please his master. A slave had no rights, no will, and no ambition other than the will and the desires of his master. Slaves were subservient and obedient.

Before I answered the call to ministry, I struggled with my own desires to climb the corporate ladder of success. I had no idea that my life was not my own to control. I grew up Baptist and in the early '70's; I wasn't exposed to preaching about fulfilling one's destiny and understanding purpose. I didn't ask God what college should I attend and what should be my major? I understood Him to be Savior, but I had yet to submit to Him as Lord. I will never forget the day I prostrated myself and cried out, "God, what have you called me to do?" He answered, "I'm glad you finally asked!" My life has changed dramatically as a result of my lining up with the will of the Father.

To Paul it was an honor to be purchased and possessed by Christ. He recognized that he existed only to serve Christ and that he had no rights of his own. As a slave of Jesus Christ, he felt honored to hold that position.

Paul Exemplified a Serving Attitude

In the first chapter of Galatians, Paul boldly addresses the believers at Galatia concerning his role as an apostle and servant-leader. "For do I now persuade men, or God? or do I seek to please men? for if I yet pleased men, I should not be the servant of Christ," (Gal 1:10). Critics of Paul and false teachers had infiltrated the churches of Galatia (Gal 1:10-16). The Judaizers were denying Paul's authority as an apostle and teaching that circumcision was necessary for salvation.

Paul asked and answered his own question by agreeing with his critics. Before his transformation he was a man-pleaser; but as a servant-leader of God, Paul boldly declared he sought to please God not men. Paul lived by the principle that Jesus declared to his disciples, "If any man serve me, let him follow me, and where I am, there shall also my servant be: if any man serve me, him will my Father honor" (John 12:26).

The Apostle Paul again came under attack by false teachers in Corinth. By the time he wrote his second epistle to the Corinthian believers his critics were more vocal in their opposition against Paul and his teachings: "For we preach not ourselves, but Christ Jesus the Lord; and ourselves your servants for Jesus sake" (2 Cor 4:5). Paul labored to advance the cause of Christ. As a servant-leader, Paul served Christ by serving the Body of Christ.

Paul Cultivated a Humble Spirit

In Phil 2:8, Paul describes the actions of Jesus as a servant-leader; "He humbled himself and became obedient unto death." This statement was made to remind the Philippian believers of the humbleness with which Jesus Christ served as their leader. The saints in Philippi had been comforting and supportive of the Apostle Paul on numerous occasions, (Phil 4:15-18l; 2 Cor 11:9). The Philippian epistle was not only written to express Paul's gratitude, but to address some of the problems in their church.

> According to Paul, to be a "servant of God" was the highest title of honor

Rivalry and personal ambition were influencing some believers. Paul reminded them that Christ set aside His deity when He became man. As a servant-leader, He took on the spirit of meekness, eliminating all self-interest (emptied), and submitted Himself to the will of the Father.

I remember the day that I found myself on my face crying out to God, "Lord, what have you called me to do?" I never asked God where I should go to college or what I should major in. Back in the seventies, most pastors were not preaching about "fulfilling one's destiny". I had no clue that God had a divine purpose for my life and it wasn't to climb the corporate ladder. I worked for a fortune 500 company, drove a new company car, and made good money, but I wasn't happy. God's assignment and my agenda were at odds! "What is your will for me I asked?" He answered, "I'm glad you finally asked, I've called you to minister.

Paul writes that there should be no discord, no divisiveness, no jealousy, no personal ambition, and no feeling of superiority in God's church. Believers are called to be serving one another according to the example set by Christ.

Let nothing be done through strife or vainglory; but in lowliness of mind let each esteem others better than themselves. Look not every man on his own things, but every man also on the things of others," (Phil 2:3,4).

Paul Exhibited a Submissive Spirit

The Apostle Paul begins his pastoral epistle to Titus by declaring his relationship to God and the Lord Jesus Christ, "Paul, a servant of God and an apostle of Jesus Christ, according to the faith of God's elect and the acknowledging of the truth which is after godliness," (Tit 1:1). His purpose, focus, and mission was to further the gospel. As a messenger of God, Paul considered himself a slave, totally submitted to serving God. He proudly proclaimed his position as a bondservant. According to Paul, to be a "servant of God" was the highest title of honor. Paul wanted Titus to know that being subservient to God was not a shameful subjection.

CHAPTER SIX

MICROWAVE PROMOTION

Contemporary Servant Leaders

The mindset of many in today's churches is that leaders are to be served based upon their conferred titles and positions. Yet biblical history has shown that the greatest men of God have always been called "servants of God" based upon their ability to serve.

> When I was in college I thought that having a title of authority meant telling people what to do; after all managers don't serve, they command

- Moses was the slave of God (Deu 34:5; Ps 105:26).
- Joshua was the slave of God (Josh 24:9).

- David was the slave of God (2 Sam 3:18; Ps 78:70).
- Paul was the slave of God (Rom 1:1; Phil 1:1; Tit 1:1).
- James was the slave of God (Jas 1:1).
- Jude was the slave of God (Jude 1).
- The prophets were the slaves of God (Amos 3:7; Jer7: 25).

When I was in college I thought that having a title with authority meant telling people what to do; after all managers don't serve, they command. That has become the mindset of many aspiring leaders in the church. There is no longer a balance between serving and being served. Church leaders must return to the biblical mandate set by Jesus Christ.

In his essay "Leadership and Power," John Gardner defines power as 'the capacity to ensure the outcomes one wishes and to prevent those one does not wish.' Today we generally equate position with power.[12]

The Bible uses the noun "servant" and the verb "serve" over 500 times. For Christians, the motivation should be serving in the name of the Lord as opposed to what can one gain from others. Nelson Price, author of, *Servants Not Celebrities*, asserts,

Few among those who are "making it" in our society

today have servant temperaments. Exaggerated egos have become our role models. Celebrity status is often sought at the expense of conviction and character. This even trickles down into the Christian's faith in subtle ways. Only when "What can I do for you" replace "What is in it for me" does one begin to grow as a fulfilled servant.[13]

Servant leaders have surrendered their egos to Christ. They reflect the fruit of the Holy Spirit outlined in Gal 5:22,23. They are not self-focused or self-serving. Author, Leighton Ford recently concluded,

We generally measure our greatness by how many supporters and helpers we have. Instead, Jesus took a child in his arms and said, "Whosoever shall receive one of such children in my name, receiveth me; and whosoever shall receive me, receiveth not me, but him that sent me." (Mark 9:37).[14]

Many equate leadership with power and greatness. Utilizing a pyramid approach, one would view the leader at the top with everyone else serving him. There is no room for top-down leadership in the church. Therefore, servant leadership has more to do with empowering those who serve than maintaining positions of greatness. Leighton Ford illustrates servant leadership,

Greatness is measured by taking the last place, by a total commitment to welcome the "little ones." Here are the

questions he gives to measure our greatness: Not "How many people help me?" but "How deep is my commitment to others?" Not "Whom do I let into the circle of influence?" but "How long and broad is my circle of fellowship? Whom can I include and still be loyal to Jesus? Not "How can I best develop myself?" but "How intense is my passion to be pure and useful?"[15]

> To be a servant of God, one must be able to say that the Christ who lives in him is also the Christ who desires to serve through him

To be effective as a servant leader you must understand the mission to which you were called. On the night that he was betrayed, Jesus made a profound statement, "For whether is greater, he that sitteth at meat or he that serveth? Is not he that sitteth at meat? But I am among you as he that serveth" (Luke 22:26).

Leighton Ford clarifies his view when states,

So Jesus says that leadership in the kingdom involves a sovereign assignment. Leadership is a call from God, not a position we choose for ourselves.[16]

Theologically, in the early Church every believer was called to serve. The theological meaning of the word did not apply to an elite group of believers. Over a period of time the verb "serve" has become a noun, "servant"   for positional-minded people whose ambition is not to serve, but to be served.

As you become a servant of God, you must make the transition from doing toward an emphasis of being. Who you are and what you do must merge to the point that by demonstration it will be obvious. To be a servant of God, one must be able to say that the Christ who lives in him is also the Christ who desires to serve through him.

"I am crucified with Christ: nevertheless I live; yet not I but Christ liveth in me: and the life which I now live in the flesh I live by the faith of the Son of God, who loved me and gave himself for me" (Gal 2:20).

In one of His teachable moments, Jesus shared with the disciples, "For even the Son of Man came not to be ministered unto, but to minister, and to give his life a ransom for many" (Mark 10:45). Servant leaders are called to imitate Christ by serving others as Christ served.

Servanthood is the opposite of the world's definition of lordship. The title Lord was used in various ways in the New Testament. Kurios, the Greek word for Lord, was used as a title of respect or for one who had authority. Jesus asked the disciples if they understood what He was doing when He demonstrated for them the example He wanted them to follow.

"Ye call me Master Lord: and ye say well; for so I am. If I then, your Lord and Master, have washed your feet; ye also ought to wash one another's feet. For I have given you an example, that ye should do as I have done to you. Verily, verily, I say unto you, The servant is not greater than his lord; neither he that is sent greater than he that sent him." (John 13:13-16).

While servant leadership does require humility, it does not require one to give up his identity. Jesus knew who He was and what His assignment was. Society would have placed Jesus in a dictatorial position of a commander who demanded allegiance of his followers.

I think it is dangerous when a leader feels, as though she has no identity apart from her title; therefore she finds her self-worth in her position.

Developing the qualities of a servant leader is difficult since the main requirement for servant leadership is self-lessness, not selfishness. According to Robert Neuschel, author of *The Servant Leader: Unleashing the Power of Your People*,

The servant leader is one who has followers whom he/she helps to grow in stature, capacity, or in some way contributes to building them into more useful and satisfied people. Not all successful manager/leaders ever become true servant leaders.[17]

The litmus test for servant leadership can be found in the leader's followers. If the leader has made an investment in his followers and has equipped them to be better leaders, he has served well.

In a society whose emphasis is performance, servant leaders are more concerned with empowering good leaders. In the tenth chapter of Mark, you will find the story of a blind man, Bartimaeus who was begging by the roadside when Jesus came by. His faith to believe that Jesus could heal him brought forth a miracle.

In his book *Transforming Leadership*, Leighton Ford contends,

Not only did the blind man receive his sight. The disciples of Jesus received their sight. They saw the vision of what made a true leader. On Jesus' way to accomplish a great thing, going to Jerusalem to die on a cross for the sins of the world, he still had time to stop for one blind man. If he went this way, who are we to go differently? Here is the heart of leadership in Christ. We do not start at the cross and go on to bigger and better things. We start there and go deeper and deeper, but there we also find the power, the living power, of the same Jesus.[18]

New Testament leadership in the twenty-first century must still resist the pressure of promoting men and women whose titles and positions produce kingdoms for themselves. Servant leaders enable followers to put to use their talents, gifts, and abilities to advance God's agenda.

CHAPTER SEVEN

WILL THE REAL LEADER PLEASE STAND UP

In the twenty-second chapter of Luke, the Bible describes the disciples jockeying for position, recognition, power, and authority. While the disciples were still thinking that Jesus was planning to establish an earthly kingdom,

> The disciples wanted to guarantee themselves of having positions of power and authority in Jesus' kingdom

Jesus took advantage of their struggle to teach them the principles of servant leadership.

New Testament leadership is not political-play (Luke 22:24). It was common in the society of that day for the highest position to sit on the right of the host and the next highest on the left. The disciples wanted to guarantee themselves of having positions of power and authority in Jesus' kingdom.

In my early days of ministry, I served in a position that placed me in the "limelight". On Sunday mornings I sat in a chair next to the senior pastor. Every time I had an outside preaching engagement, the other ministers "rushed" toward my chair, hoping that they would have the opportunity to sit in it.

New Testament leadership is not an authoritarian attitude (Luke 22:25). Negative connotations are attributed to the world's definition of greatness. Their concept of greatness is holding authority over people or lording over them. The worldly benefactor wants to be recognized, known, and honored for his contribution. His motives are purely selfish. "And whosoever shall exalt himself shall be abased; and he that shall humble himself shall be exalted," (Matt 23:12).

New Testament leadership is not cultic control (Luke 2:26,27). Jesus was not opposed to men holding positions of greatness or authority. His concept of greatness involved esteeming and serving others. The chief position was that of a servant, "Let nothing be done through strife or vainglory; but in lowliness of mind let each esteem others better than themselves," (Phil 2:3).

What then is a servant leader? Leadership is not a science, it is an art; therefore, it can be interpreted in numerous ways. Most definitions of leadership focus more on what a leader does than who he is. The foundation of leadership is influence. Leaders are called to influence the lives of others. While leadership can be defined as the ability to make things happen through people, a servant leader develops and empowers followers.

J. Oswald Sanders, author of *Spiritual Leadership*, asserts,

Many people regard leaders as naturally gifted with intellect, personal forcefulness, and enthusiasm. Such qualities certainly enhance leadership potential, but they do not define the spiritual leader.[19]

Biblical leadership must be specific and scriptural. Jesus criticized the religious leaders of His day because they had become hypocrites (Matt 23:1-39). They had intellectual knowledge but they lacked spiritual wisdom and application; therefore, they could not lead others.

In the Old Testament, a leader was a servant of God and His people. The portrait of a biblical leader is one who is under authority to the will of God. He receives, obeys, and executes the commands of God. He models the will of God by being in the forefront.

Servant leadership takes place when three main qualities exist.

- A leader must sense a call by God to be a servant. Leaders are called to serve by demonstration.

- A leader must be Christ-like in character.

- A servant leader must be able to guide and empower people to complete their mission.

Leadership guru, Robert Greenleaf, defends his position by stating,

My thesis, that more servants should emerge as leaders, or should follow only servant leaders, is not a popular one. It is much more comfortable to go with a less demanding point of view about what is expected of one now.[20]

According to J. Oswald Sanders, to be a servant leader in the church one must be authoritative, spiritual, and sacrificial, possessing strength and supernatural faith. In his book *The Making of a Christian Leader*, Ted Engstrom, declares,

Men of faith have always been men of action. It is impossibility for active men to serve in a passive Role. This implies that such people are decisive in Nature. Leadership demands faith. The setting of and striving for goals is an act of faith.[21]

God has provided certain principles in His Word as a

foundation for church leadership. The believer's greatest example of a servant leader is Jesus, whose ministry focused on leadership development.

The leadership of Jesus focused on individuals as He attempted to pour His life into them while transforming them into disciples. His leadership focused on the Word of God as the foundation for training, empowering, and serving. The leadership of Jesus focused on Himself as the mediator between God and mankind. He understood His assignment, He knew His mission was short, and He realized His task was to reproduce Himself in the lives of others who would complete His work.

CHAPTER EIGHT

CAN YOU PASS THE TEST?

The Apostle Paul provided a character test for leadership in his letters to both Timothy and Titus. In Timothy 3:1-13 and Titus 1:5-9, the Bible provides an extensive list of qualifications that should be used to measure the character and maturity of potential servant leaders.

We live in a society that operates according to standards. Most corporate job positions are filled based upon individuals meeting minimum standards. There are too many Christians who believe their talents should make room for them "regardless to their lifestyle".

Many of the instructions that Paul gave Timothy concerning the recruitment of deacons should also be used in recruiting servant leaders today; "And let these also first be proved; then let them use the office of a deacon, being found blameless, (1 Tim 3:10). In 2 Timothy 2:2, Paul further commands Timothy to commit the Word to faithful servants.

Author, Laurie Beth Jones affirms,

The principle of service is what separates true leaders from glory seekers. Jesus, the leader, served his people. Most religions teach that we are put here to serve God; yet in Jesus, God is offering to serve us.[22]

A leader is to be an example to the flock; therefore he must be above reproach, having unquestionable integrity (1 Tim 3:2; Tit 1:7). He is required to manage his home well by being a faithful husband and a self controlled, nonviolent, disciplined, and even-tempered man (1 Tim 3:2,3; Tit 1:6-8). In addition, he must possess good judgment, have a respectable lifestyle, and not be self-pleasing, arrogant, or contentious (1 Tim 3:2, 3; Tit 1:7). He must also be open to receiving guests in his home, have a good reputation with those outside the church, and have the ability to teach (1 Tim 3:2, 7; Tit 1:6). As a devout man, he must be just in his dealings and not greedy concerning money (Tit 1:8, 1 Tim 3:3). Finally, he must be rooted in the Scriptures; therefore, he cannot be a novice (Tit 1:9; 1 Tim 3:6).

CHAPTER NINE

SERVANT LEADER:

ATTITUDE ADJUSTMENT

One aspect of leadership that was not mentioned above is a godly attitude. Attitude can be defined as one's character, deposition, frame of mind, position, perspective, or temperament. Psalm 100:2 commands one to "Serve the Lord with gladness." Serving God equates to serving one another.

Servant leaders are "servant" conscious and therefore "service" conscious. According to the Apostle Peter,

"And above all things have fervent charity among yourselves: for charity shall cover the multitude of sins. Use hospitality one to another without grudging. As every man hath received the gift, even so minister (serve) the same one to another, as good stewards of the manifold grace of God.

If any man speak, let him speak as the oracles of God; if any man minister (serve), let him do it as of the ability which God giveth: that God in Christ, to whom be praise and dominion forever and ever" (1 Pet 4:8-11).

Servant leaders are to serve with a loving and forgiving attitude. The word "fervent" is an athletic word that means to stretch or reach out. Servant leaders are called to reach out in the same manner that Jesus reached when He introduced the disciples to a new command.

> Serving God equates to serving one another

"A new commandment I give you, that ye love one another as I have loved you, that ye also love one another. By this shall all men know that ye are my disciples (servants), if ye have love to another" (John 13:34,35).

The attitude of a servant leader will determine how he uses his gifts to serve and empower the Body of Christ. The word gift means special ability given to the servant by God. Servant leaders should aspire to use their gifts serving and ministering to others: "As we have therefore opportunity, let us do good unto all men, especially unto them who are of the household of faith" (Gal 6:10).

So important is one's attitude that Samuel Logan Brengle wrote:

*One of the outstanding ironies of history is the utter dis-
regard of ranks and titles in the final judgments men pass
on each other. The final estimate of men shows that history
cares not an iota for the rank or title a man has borne, or
the office he has held, but only the quality of his deeds and
the character of his mind and heart.*[23]

Servant leaders are called to serve one another as good
stewards. A steward was a slave who was given the responsibility of the master's property. His mentality was to be
faithful as a servant. Likewise, a servant leader's disposi-
tion must be to serve faithfully in the position that he is
given, "Moreover it is required in stewards, that a man be
found faithful" (1 Cor 4:2).

CHAPTER TEN

TITLE AND POSITION OR PERFORMANCE AND PRODUCTIVITY

Society is crying out for effective leaders. However, there is a difference between "leadership" and "the leader." The leader is the person who assumes the position and accepts the responsibility to lead; leadership is functioning in the designated position. According to Myles Monroe, "In essence, a title and a position do not guarantee performance and productivity." Leighton Ford stated,

As I understand Jesus, his bottom line was not just getting the job done, but growing people and getting the job done. It has been said that transformational leaders work themselves out of a job, as subordinates are converted into leaders.[24]

As a servant leader, Jesus recognized the importance of

empowering leadership. His leadership influenced not only His disciples, but also the multitude that followed Him. Throughout the Gospels, Jesus portrays Himself as a trainer, a mentor, and a teacher, which affirms His effectiveness as a servant leader. His transforming process of leadership was completed in stages.

- He met them and recruited them to become disciples.

- He mentored them, spending intimate time with them.

- He became a model for them by setting the example by which they should follow.

- He sent them out and monitored their progress.

- He expected them to reproduce themselves in others.

The final stage would be the litmus test of His effectiveness. The disciples' ability to go forth and multiply and reproduce the cycle was a determining factor in Jesus' effectiveness as a servant leader.

"Henceforth I call you not servants; for the servant knoweth not what his lord doeth: but I have called you friends; for all things that I have heard of my Father I have made known unto you," (John 15:15).

CHAPTER ELEVEN

DO YOU HAVE WHAT IT TAKES?

There are numerous ways to measure a person's progress. Renowned author, Warren Wiersbe, affirms,

> *God is glorified when people see the Lord and not the servant: "Let your light so shine before me, that they may see your good works and glorify your Father in heaven" (Matt 5:16). You have to decide whether you will be a servant or a celebrity, whether you will magnify Christ or promote yourself (Phil 1:20,21).*[25]

When gauging a person's development, consider the following questions. Do the person's talents, gifts, and abilities match the position for which he is being considered?

There are times when an individual is placed in a vacated position to fill a need. For maximum development, servant leaders should be placed in areas in which they are strong. Does the person demonstrate consistency in her present position? People often start out energetic but they lack stick-to-itiveness. In addition, can the potential leader's involvement in an organization be concretely evaluated? Excuses or unprofitable activity cannot camouflage productivity.

Another question to be answered is, How effective have they been in handling adversity and difficult situations? The call to servant leadership requires fortitude.

An important question not to be overlooked is, Have they demonstrated that they can submit themselves to authority and follow the chain of command? The mandate for biblical leadership is submission; the call to serve requires obedience.

Finally, if they found themselves placed in a position to work under the leadership of someone whom they felt had less knowledge or experience, how did they react? One's attitude will determine one's altitude.

God prepared most of the leaders in the Bible before He ever began to use them. Each leader was trained differently and their preparation time varied. Paul wrote in 1 Timothy 3:10, "But let these also first be tested; then let them serve as deacons, being found blameless." God uses specific tests to try the attitude and motives of leaders. These tests accomplish several things:

- The test equips the leader with spiritual understanding.

- The test removes bitterness and selfishness from the leader's heart.

- The test produces faithfulness within the leader.

- The test confirms the call upon the leader's life.

Every Christian must have a measure of faith in God; however, a leader's faith must be highly developed. Storms, disappointments, and crises are just a few of the tools God uses to process leaders. The test of faith will always challenge a leader to trust in God. God tested Abraham's faith twice concerning Isaac. At the age of seventy-five he was promised a son; at the age of one hundred his son was born. Years later his faith was again tested when he offered his son as a living sacrifice. Today, Abraham is still considered the Father of faith.

A leader's character will always be tested to determine the area of weakness in his personality. In order to develop leaders with strong, godly character, God will test their motives and ability to submit to His will. Joseph was tested in prison and in Potiphar's house. His exemplary character pleased God and he was later promoted.

An effective leader must be emotionally stable and able to handle tension, frustration, and conflict. An emotionally mature leader will exhibit the following characteristic: sensitivity, trust, confidence, tolerance, loyalty, and sympathy. Mature leaders are creative and innovative and have the ability to motivate others. God called Moses His friend; a man who spent forty years on the back side of a mountain and forty years in the wilderness leading a rebellious people to the promised land.

Mature leaders are trustworthy, disciplined, confident, decisive, courageous, and unselfish. From the time of his conversion, the Apostle Paul went through numerous tests: prison, shipwreck, and physical abuse. His promotion as a leader was based upon his ability to faithfully serve the will of God.

In addition, God will test a leader's ability to serve others and to submit to those who have authority. Elisha left his profession and faithfully served Elijah. He was later promoted to become Elijah's successor.

To develop a leader to maturity, God stretches him in the area of spiritual warfare. Effective leaders know the voice of God and can operate in prayer and warfare. Daniel was a man of prayer who entered into a spiritual battle for twenty-one days before receiving his answer from God.

Then God gave him favor and promoted him in the eyes of men.

The Bible illustrates what it takes to be an effective servant leader. Both good and bad leadership models are mentioned, from great men like Abraham, Moses, David, and Paul, to failing kings like Saul and Herod.

These are the crucial questions that must be honestly answered when considering individuals for servant leadership positions. Enormous struggles arise when churches fail to recognize the importance of proving leaders before conferring upon them titles and positions of authority. Leaders who behave like dictators encounter resistance, dissension, and sometimes rebellion as a result of their actions. The test of effective servant leadership is whether the leader can say to the followers: "Ye know what manner of men we were among you for your sake. And ye became followers of us, and of the Lord" (1 Thess 1:5-6). Leadership is tested and authenticated by how one serves, not by how one dictates.

How then should potential servant leaders be chosen? Scripture outlines how servant leadership should be fulfilled in the church. The Apostle Paul exhorts Timothy to first prove leaders before setting them before the people (1 Tim 3:10).

To be promoted into servant leadership, one must

demonstrate several characteristics.

- · God looks for individuals who have surrendered their will to His will. Every leader must be able to die to his personal ambitions in order to complete his assignment. God will test a leader to determine what is in his heart.

- · A servant leader must have self-control and discipline.

- · He must be stable and steadfast.

- · It is important that a leader be spiritually balanced.

- · A servant leader must operate in wisdom.

- · A leader must have sound judgment. Leaders are called to be fair-minded, practical, and conscientious.

According to Titus 1:8, a potential leader must not only have right standing with God, but he must also deal honestly with others. He must practice righteousness. God also views faithfulness and consistency as characteristics worthy of promotion.

Another trait necessary for effective leadership is faithfulness to the Word of God. A servant leader must be able to interpret God's Word, discern God's voice, and lead God's people. A successful leader cannot be double minded or easily moved.

Successful leaders are able to view disappointments as opportunities. A good leader has the ability to stay calm in a crisis. When Jesus and the disciples were out in a boat during a storm, Jesus established His leadership by staying calm in the midst of the storm. When Moses and the children of Israel were at the Red Sea, the people panicked but Moses remained calm and obeyed the command of God.

According to author Hans Finzel,

A servant leader sees his or her role quite differently from the traditional top-down dictator type. The servant leader is there to make the worker successful, not vise versa. Our workers and/or employees are hired to serve not us, but the mission of our church or organization. Our role as their leaders is to facilitate their effectiveness in any way we can, much as a coach tries to get optimum performance out of his team players.[26]

Outstanding leaders inspire confidence by demonstrating faithfulness over little assignments. Cultivating a driving vision is a foundational key toward servant leadership. When followers see that a leader is committed to the vision, they too become committed. A leader with a clear purpose is persistent even in the face of setbacks and failures.

CHAPTER TWELVE

NO TURNING BACK:

THE CALL TO COMMITMENT

Servant leadership demands commitment. One problem that continues to magnify itself in leadership is a lack of stick-to-itiveness. The problem centers in a lack of understanding of the responsibility that accompanies the title and position of servant leadership.

On several occasions Jesus emphasized the repercussions for serving Him. In Mattew 10:32,33, Jesus told His disciples that if they denied Him before men, He would deny them before His Father in heaven. In Luke 14:26,27, He demanded loyalty over father, mother, sister, brother, wife, children, and even one's self. He taught them to deny themselves (Matt 16:24) and to carry their crosses (Matt 10:38).

In the sixth chapter of the Book of John, the Apostle John describes how many of the disciples who followed Jesus became disgruntled and turned away. According to Fred Smith, "The only way people will perform excellently over the long-term is if they fully comprehend what they are doing."

The problem of recruiting servant leaders who are willing to go the distance is not a new challenge. Jesus faced the disappointment of pouring Himself into followers whose commitment fizzled at the thought of hardship. His language and methods were severe because He did not want half-committed servants. He recognized His time on earth was short and that it was His responsibility to draw true servant leaders to complete the work He began.

Personal sacrifice is not very popular according to John F. MacArthur, author of *The Gospel According to Jesus*,

The idea of daily self-denial does not jive with the contemporary supposition that believing in Jesus is a momentary decision. A true believer is one who signs up for life. The bumper-sticker sentiment, "Try Jesus," is a mentality foreign to real discipleship--This is not an experiment, but a lifelong commitment.[27]

Jesus placed demands on His servant leaders long before He promoted them and gave them positions of authority to establish the church. While multitudes followed Jesus at a distance, only those willing to submit themselves to the rigorous training passed the test.

After these things the Lord appointed other seventy also, and sent them two and two before his face into every city and place, whither he himself would come. Therefore said he unto them, "The harvest truly is great, but the laborers are few: pray ye therefore the Lord of the harvest, that he would send forth laborers into his harvest. Go your ways: behold, I send you forth as lambs among wolves," (Luke 10:1-3).

As the standard for leadership increased, the number of qualified leaders decreased and Jesus found himself ministering more to the twelve and at times to His inner circle of three and ultimately giving final instructions to the one.

According to respected author, Robert Clinton,

Not all leaders finish well. I have observed four patterns concerning the response of leaders to processing the ministry development phrase. The pattern includes: (1) drop outs--quite a few, (2) plateaued leaders--the majority of leaders, (3) disciplined--a few, and (4) those who continued to grow and finish well--some. The challenge is to finish well, as the Apostle Paul did.[28]

The last words of the greatest servant leader, Jesus were, "It is finished" (John 19:30). "I have glorified thee on the earth: I have finished the work which thou gavest me to do" (John 17:4). How did Jesus glorify the Father? He finished the work that God had given Him. The reason that Jesus was ready to be gloried was that He had glorified the Father by staying faithful to the end.

CHAPTER THIRTEEN

CONCLUSION

The entire ministry of Jesus was based upon leadership, "As the Father has sent Me, and I also send you" (John 20:21). In a most memorable demonstration of servant leadership, Jesus modeled with a towel and basin what He envisioned leadership to be: humbling oneself to serve another. To the disciples, foot washing was humiliating; but to the Master it was the job description of a servant.

"For I have given you an example that ye should do as I have done to you. Verily, verily, I say unto you, The servant is not greater than his lord; neither he that is sent greater than he that sent him. If ye know these things, happy are ye if ye do them" (John 13:15-17).

The leadership of Jesus focused on individuals as He

attempted to pour His life into them while transforming them into His disciples. His leadership focused on the Word of God as the foundation for training, empowering, and serving. He understood His assignment; He knew His mission was short, and He realized His task was to reproduce Himself in the lives of others who would complete His work.

The mark of a servant leader is his ability to effectively influence and empower his followers. Jesus demonstrated His effectiveness as a leader by returning to His position in Heaven. He was so confident in what He had accomplished that He transferred His power and authority to His followers.

The Apostle Paul began three of his epistles with the salutation: "Paul, a servant of Jesus Christ" (Rom 1:1), "Paul and Timotheus, the servants of Jesus Christ" (Phil 1:1), and "Paul, a servant of God" (Tit 1:1). Paul's message was a pure gospel. His motive was not to please men, but God. He was not motivated by greed, glory, or popularity, "For we do not preach ourselves, but Christ Jesus the Lord, and ourselves your bondservants for Jesus' sake" (2 Cor 4:5).

When writing the church at Philippi, Paul outlined his philosophy of leadership: Let this mind be in you, which was also in Christ Jesus: Who, being in the form of God, thought it not robbery to be equal with God but made himself of no reputation, and took upon him the form of a servant, and was made in the likeness of men (Phil 2:5-7).

Potential servant leaders should note that the biblical concept of leadership is contrary to the leadership philosophy of this secular society. Sadly, many Christian organizations have adopted the world-view of leadership: followers serve leaders; the more who serve the leader, the greater the leader. Spiritual leadership positions were never intended to be positions of dominance or control. Servant leaders exist to empower the organization. Servant leadership at its best is "leading by serving."

According to Dr. Myles Monroe,

You must assess your personal motivation for leadership. Are you willing to serve? Are you willing to be patient? Are you willing to say, "I'm available?" You may be available, but are you prepared for the cost and price of leadership? Nevertheless, some people come into leadership with tremendous zeal and little understanding of the dynamics involved.[29]

These are the crucial questions that must be honestly answered when considering individuals for servant leadership positions. Enormous struggles arise when churches fail to recognize the importance of proving leaders before conferring upon them titles and positions of authority. Leaders who behave like dictators encounter resistance, dissension, and sometimes rebellion as a result of their actions.

The test of effective servant leadership is whether the leader can say to the followers: "Ye know what manner of men we were among you for your sake. And ye became followers of us, and of the Lord" (1 Thess 1:5-6). Leadership is tested and authenticated by how one serves, not by how one dictates.

AFTERWORD
DR. LAFAYETTE SCALES

There are many complex paradoxes in the development of a leader. How to be powerful yet touchable? How to focus on personal goals yet be a team player? How to be a servant leader? The tension between these concepts have caused many leaders to conclude that they can be either powerful or touchable.

They can achieve personal goals or team goals. They can be a servant or a leader. These perplexities are not settled by the either/or paradigm but rather by the both/and view. Many potentially great leaders draw many permanent conclusions too early, based on contemporary models which may have distorted truths that would help shape a great leader. Do you remember when politicians used to be called public servants? In many nations, national leaders are known as Minister of Education, Ministers of Defense, Ministers of Finance. These are not titles but descriptions of public service.

My model for leadership, the Lord Jesus Christ, says greatness is achieved by service. He demonstrated greatness by serving, not by being served. The greatest leader was known for His service. Great servants become great leaders with proper instruction, opportunity and preparation. Great leaders never forget it is their service that produces their greatness. Your service will make you great.

The McDonalds Corporation is great because it serves a reliable fast food product all over the world. Microsoft is great because it serves its clients with the software and support necessary to stay on the technological cutting edge. Starbucks is great because it serves the public consistent coffee products. All of these corporations are servant leaders in their industry. Take away the service from any of these enterprises, and they will fail.

In our kingdom we are servant leaders. Dr. Gaither has set forth a balanced approach to leadership. The commitment to this balanced approach in leadership creates a healthy tension. Servant leaders willing to walk in this healthy tension, produce a kingdom model that gives an alternative to the skewed contemporary models we now see. This model is consistent with the original intent of the creator who called servants to lead.

I encourage you to read the truths, principles and precepts of this book over and over again until your mind is renewed, your life is transformed and there is manifestation of these truths in your life as a servant leader.

Apostle La Fayette Scales
Senior Pastor
Rhema Christian Center
Columbus, Ohio

NOTES

[1] Laurie Beth Jones, <u>Jesus CEO</u> (New York: Hyperion, 1995), 241.

[2] John C. Maxwell, <u>Developing the Leaders Around You</u> (Nashville: Thomas Nelson, Inc., 1995), 39.

[3] Kortright Davis, <u>Serving with Power</u> (New York: Paulist Press, 1999), 128.

[4] Hans Finzel, <u>Empowered Leaders</u> (Nashville: Word Publishing, 1998), xvii.

[5] Ibid., 22.

[6] Jim McGuiggan, <u>The God of the Towel</u> (West Monroe, LA: Howard Publishing Co.), 141.

[7] Gayle D. Erwin, <u>The Jesus Style</u> (Waco: Word Book, 1983), 55.

[8] T. W. Mason, <u>The Servant-Messiah</u> (Grand Rapids: Baker Book House, 1980), 73.

[9] Frank Damazio, <u>The Making of a Leader</u> (Portland: Bible Temple Publishing, 1988), 81

[10] Jim McGuiggan, <u>The God of the Towel</u> (West Monroe, LA: Howard Publishing Co., 1997), 136.

[11] Erwin, 130.

[12.] Leighton Ford, <u>Transforming Leadership</u> (Downers Grove, IL: InterVarsity Press, 1991), 141.

[13.] Nelson Price, <u>Servants Not Celebrities</u> (Nashville: Broadman Press, 1989), 10.

[14.] Ford, 145.

[15.] Ford, 148.

[16.] Ibid., 150.

[17.] Robert P. Neuschel, <u>The Servant Leader: Unleashing the Power of Your People</u> (East Lansing, MI: Vision Sports Management Group, Inc., 1998), 135.

[18.] Ford, 157.

[19.] J. Oswald Sanders, <u>Spiritual Leadership</u> (Chicago: Moody Press, 1994), 18.

[20.] Robert K. Greenleaf, <u>Servant Leadership</u> (New York: Paulist Press, 1991) 10.

[21.] Ted W. Engstrom, <u>The Making of A Christian Leader</u> (Grand Rapids: The Zondervan Company, 1976), 20-21.

[22.] Jones, 250.

[23.] Engstrom, 103.

[24.] Ford, 164.

[25.] Warren Wiersbe, <u>On Being a Servant of God</u> (Grand Rapids: Baker Books, 1993), 20.

[26.] Finzel, 41.

[27.] John F. MacArthur, Jr., <u>The Gospel According to Jesus</u> (Grand Rapids: Academie Books, 1988), 202.

[28.] Clinton, 201.

[29.] Myles Monroe, <u>Becoming a Leader</u>, (Bakerfield: Pneuma Life Publishing, 1993), 59.